NEW YORK
YANKEES

STARS, STATS, HISTORY, AND MORE!

BY K. C. KELLEY

The Child's World®
childsworld.com

Published by The Child's World®
1980 Lookout Drive • Mankato, MN 56003-1705
800-599-READ • www.childsworld.com

ISBN 9781503828322
LCCN 2018944846

Printed in the United States of America
PAO2392

Photo Credits:
Cover: Joe Robbins (2).
Interior: AP Images: David Goldman 10, Mark Lennihan
17, Elise Amendola 19; Dreamstime.com: Lenngphotog 14;
Newscom: John Angelillo/UPI 5; Joe Robbins 6, 9, 13, 23,
24, 27, 29; Shutterstock: Daniel Silva 20.

About the Author

K.C. Kelley is a huge sports
fan who has written more
than 100 books for kids. His
favorite sport is baseball.
He has also written about
football, basketball, soccer,
and even auto racing! He lives
in Santa Barbara, California.

On the Cover
Main photo: Home run hero Aaron
Judge
Inset: baseball legend Babe Ruth

CONTENTS

GO, YANKEES!

The New York Yankees are the most famous team in baseball. They have won more **World Series** than any other team. They have had more **Hall of Fame** players than any other team. The Yankees were not always so great. In 1920, they added a player named Babe Ruth. The Yanks have been the best ever since. Let's meet the Yankees!

Aaron Judge and Brett Gardner celebrate another Yankees home run! ➤

5

WHO ARE THE YANKEES?

The Yankees play in the American League (AL). That group is part of Major League Baseball (MLB). MLB also includes the National League (NL). There are 30 teams in MLB. The winner of the AL plays the winner of the NL in the World Series. The Yankees have won more World Series than any other team. They last won in 2009. That gave them a total of 27!

◄ *Aroldis Chapman can throw a baseball more than 100 miles per hour!*

WHERE THEY CAME FROM

The Yankees began as the Baltimore Orioles. That was a different Orioles team than the one that plays today. It's confusing! In 1903, Baltimore's team moved to New York City. The team joined the AL as the Highlanders. In 1913, the team changed its name to Yankees. That is a nickname for people who come from America. The Yankees play in a part of New York City called the Bronx. The team is sometimes called the Bronx Bombers!

Babe Ruth played for the Yankees from 1920 to ➤
1934. He led the team to four championships.

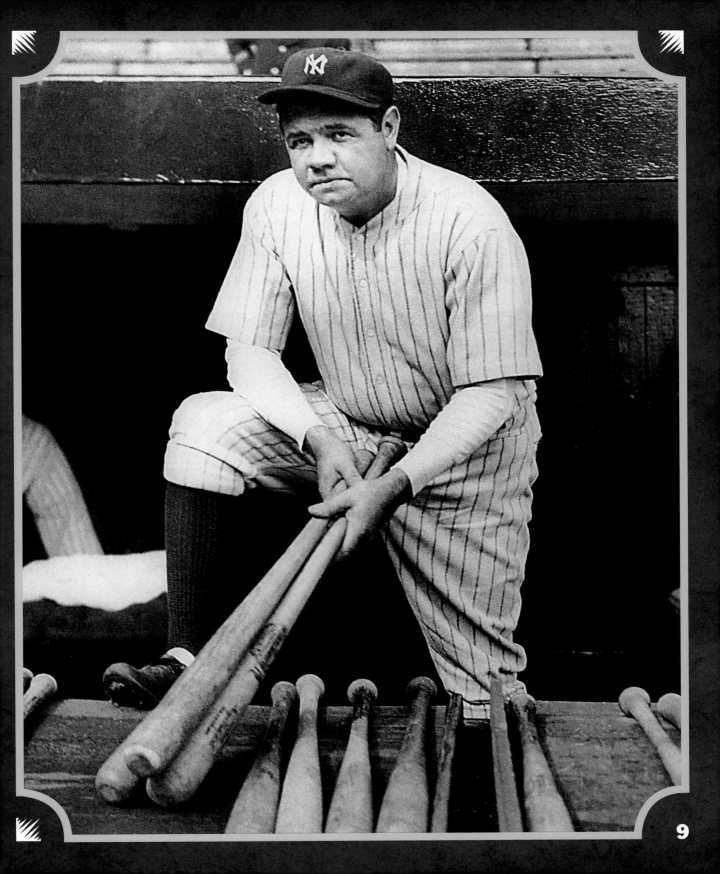

WHO THEY PLAY

The Yankees play in the AL East Division. The other teams in the AL East are the Baltimore Orioles, the Boston Red Sox, the Tampa Bay Rays, and the Toronto Blue Jays. The Yankees play more games against their division **rivals** than against other teams. In all, the Yanks play 162 games each season. They play 81 games at home and 81 on the road. Their biggest rivals are the Red Sox.

← *Yankees-Red Sox games are always very intense!*

WHERE THEY PLAY

The first Yankee Stadium opened in 1923. It was called "The House That Ruth Built." The great player Babe Ruth starred for the Yankees then. The stadium was great, but it got old. In 2009, the team opened a new Yankee Stadium. It was built next to where the old ballpark stood. Yankee Stadium is one of the largest ballparks in MLB.

The new Yankee Stadium is one of baseball's biggest. ➤

THE BASEBALL FIELD

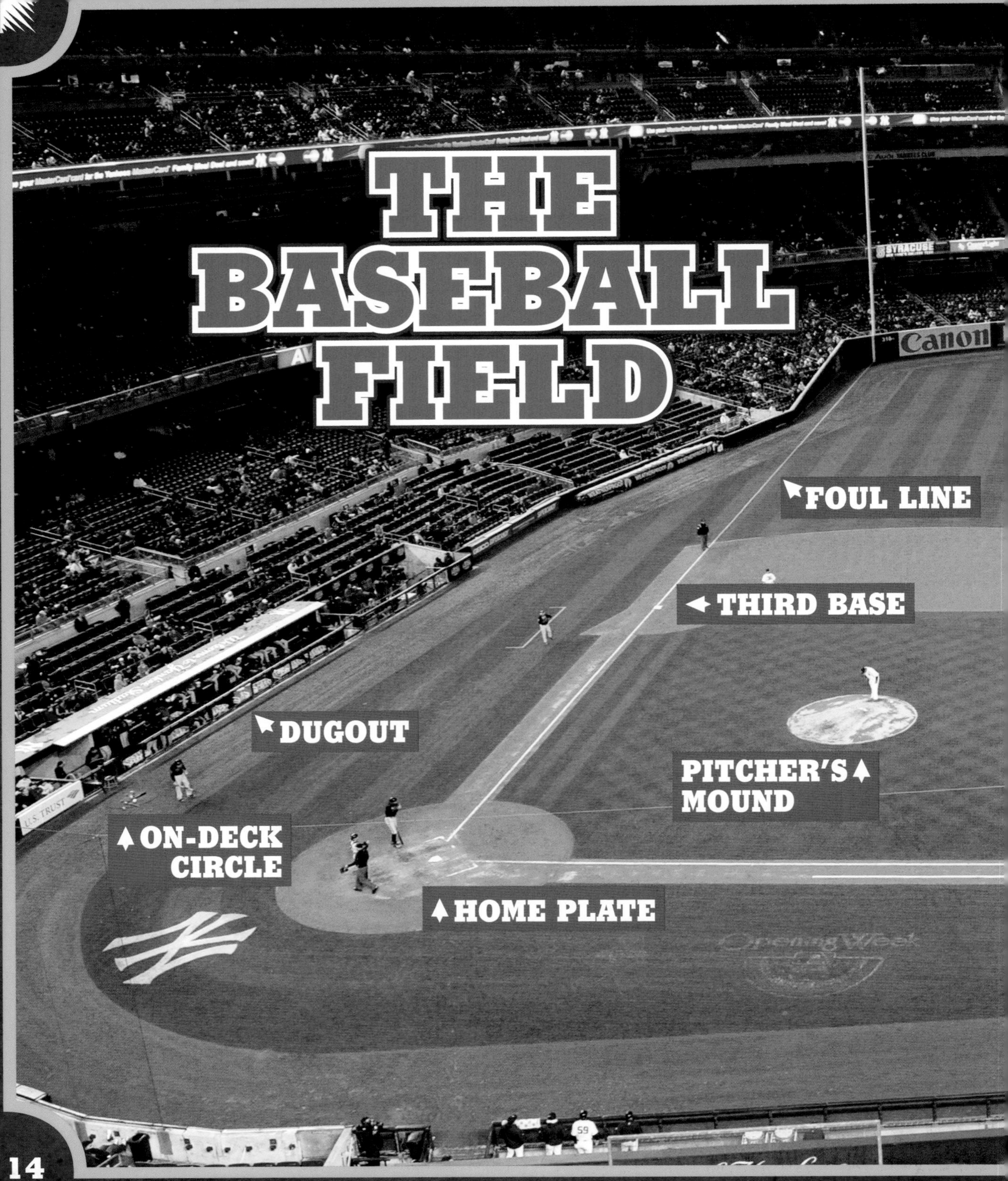

FOUL LINE

THIRD BASE

DUGOUT

PITCHER'S MOUND

ON-DECK CIRCLE

HOME PLATE

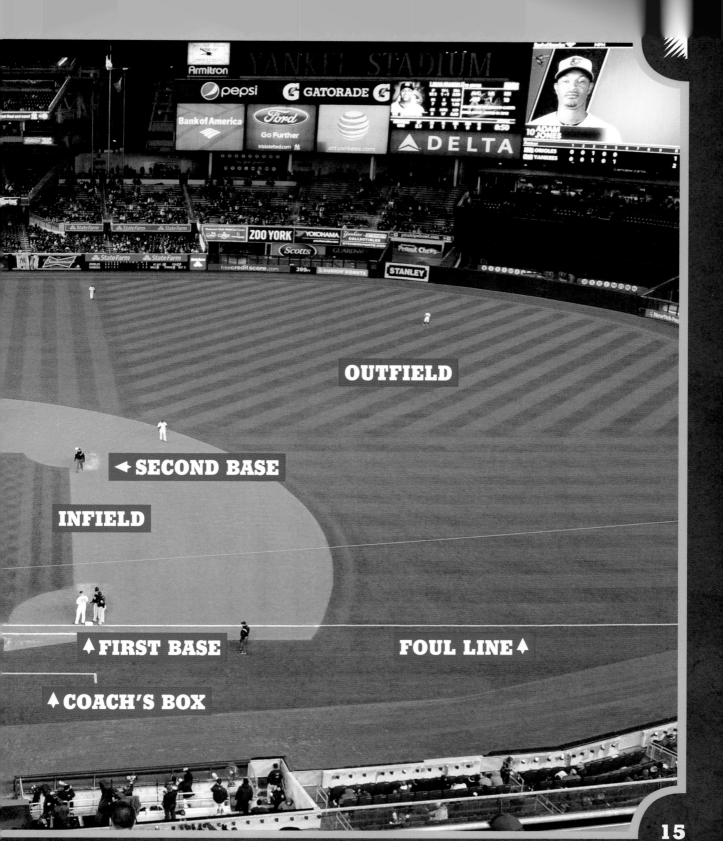

OUTFIELD

◄ SECOND BASE

INFIELD

▲ FIRST BASE

FOUL LINE ▲

▲ COACH'S BOX

BIG DAYS

The Yankees have had a lot of great days in their long history. Here are a few of them.

1927—Led by Babe Ruth and Lou Gehrig, the Yankees had one of the best teams ever. They won the World Series in four straight games.

1996—The Yankees had gone 17 years without a World Series title. That was their longest streak since 1923. The streak ended with a title this year.

2000—The Yankees share New York City with the Mets. This year, the two teams met in the "Subway Series." The Yankees won!

John Wetteland was at the center of the ➤
celebration when the Yankees won in 1996.

TOUGH DAYS

Like every team, the Yankees have had some not-so-great days, too. Here are a few their fans might not want to recall.

1908—As the Highlanders, the team was not very good. They lost 103 games this year. That was the most the club has ever lost in one season.

1980s—Things were pretty wild in the Bronx. Owner George Steinbrenner loved firing **managers**. He hired and **fired** manager Billy Martin five times!

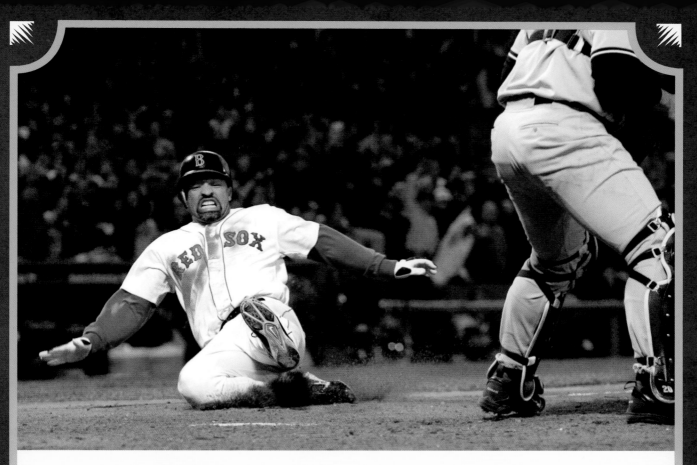

▲ *Boston's Dave Roberts slides in with the tying run in Game 4 of the 2004 ALCS. The Red Sox came back to win!*

2004—The Yankees won three straight games over the Red Sox in the playoffs. Then Boston came back to win four in a row. They beat the Yankees. It was the first time any team had come back from three games behind!

LOU GEHRIG
UNIFORM NUMBER RETIRED: 1939

LOU WAS ONE OF THE
MOST PROLIFIC YANKEES
HITTERS OF ALL TIME.
FROM 1923-1939, HIS SKILLS
AND INNER STRENGTH
WERE THINGS OF BEAUTY
ON THE BALLFIELD, EARNING HIM
THE NICKNAME "THE IRON HORSE."

BABE RUTH
UNIFORM NUMBER RETIRED: 1948

FROM 1920-1934, THE BABE
SINGLE-HANDEDLY LIFTED BASEBALL
TO NEW HEIGHTS WITH HIS
UNLIMITED TALENT AND
UNBRIDLED LOVE FOR THE GAME.
HIS ENORMOUS CONTRIBUTIONS
TO BASEBALL AND THE YANKEES
MADE HIM THE MOST CELEBRATED
ATHLETE WHO EVER LIVED

JOE DIMAG

MEET THE FANS!

Fans at Yankee Stadium enjoy a trip to the past. The team has built Monument Park to honor its heroes. Fans can see **plaques** of 38 people. That includes players, managers, and team owners. There is even a plaque for a stadium announcer! The Yankees and their fans really love the team's great history.

◄ *The numbers of Yankees greats are on display at Monument Park, including Lou Gehrig (4), Babe Ruth (3), and Joe DiMaggio (5).*

HEROES THEN

You could fill a book with stories of all the Yankees greats. The best player of all time is Babe Ruth. He was a star pitcher for Boston before becoming a home run hero for New York. He played with first baseman Lou Gehrig. Gehrig played in 2,130 straight games! Joe DiMaggio came along next. He once got a hit in 56 straight games. Mickey Mantle slugged homers and stole bases. Catcher Yogi Berra was part of 10 World Series championship teams. More recently, shortstop Derek Jeter helped New York win five titles. Mariano Rivera was probably the best **closer** ever.

Derek Jeter had more than 3,000 hits in his career. ➤

HEROES NOW

Today's Bronx Bombers live up to their name. Their lineup is packed with sluggers. Andrew Judge set a **rookie** record in 2017 with 52 homers. Giancarlo Stanton joined the team in 2018 to make a powerful one-two punch. Catcher Gary Sanchez is a top young star. Pitcher Luis Severino made his first All-Star team in 2018. Aroldis Chapman's pitches often top 100 miles per hour!

◄ *Aaron Judge is one of the Yankees' great young sluggers.*

GEARING UP

Baseball players wear team uniforms. On defense, they wear leather gloves to catch the ball. As batters, they wear hard helmets. This protects them from pitches. Batters hit the ball with long wood bats. Each player chooses his own size of bat. Catchers have the toughest job. They wear a lot of protection.

THE BASEBALL

The outside of the Major League baseball is made from cow leather. Two leather pieces shaped like 8s are stitched together. There are 108 stitches of red thread. These stitches help players grip the ball. Inside, the ball has a small center of cork and rubber. Hundreds of feet of yarn are tightly wound around this center.

CATCHER'S MASK AND HELMET

CHEST PROTECTOR ➤

WRIST BANDS ↗

▲ CATCHER'S MITT

SHIN GUARDS ➤

CATCHER'S GEAR

TEAM STATS

Here are some of the all-time career records for the New York Yankees. All these stats are through the 2018 regular season.

HOME RUNS	
Babe Ruth	659
Mickey Mantle	536

RBI	
Lou Gehrig	1,995
Babe Ruth	1,978

BATTING AVERAGE	
Babe Ruth	.349
Lou Gehrig	.340

STOLEN BASES	
Derek Jeter	358
Rickey Henderson	326

WINS	
Whitey Ford	236
Red Ruffing	231

STRIKEOUTS	
Andy Pettite	2,020
Whitey Ford	1,956

Mariano Rivera was one of the best relief pitchers of all time. ➤

SAVES	
Mariano Rivera	652
Dave Righetti	224

GLOSSARY

closer (KLO-zer) a pitcher who comes in to get the final few outs of a close game

fired (FYRD) told someone that they no longer had their job

Hall of Fame (HALL UV FAYM) a building in Cooperstown, New York, that honors famous baseball players

manager (MAN-uh-jer) the person in charge of the baseball team on the field; he chooses lineups and picks pitchers

plaques (PLAKS) plates hung on a wall that honor people or events

rivals (RYE-vuhlz) two people or groups competing for the same thing

rookie (RUH-kee) a player in his or her first season of professional sports

World Series (WURLD SEE-reez) the annual championship of Major League Baseball

FIND OUT MORE

IN THE LIBRARY

Fishman, Jon M. *Aaron Judge: Sports All-Stars*. Minneapolis, MN: Lerner, 2018.

Herman, Gail. *Who Is Derek Jeter?* New York, NY: Penguin Workshop, 2015.

Williams, Doug. *12 Reasons to Love the New York Yankees*. Mankato, MN: 12-Story Publishing, 2015.

ON THE WEB

Visit our website for links about the New York Yankees: **childsworld.com/links**

Note to Parents, Teachers, and Librarians: We routinely verify our web links to make sure they are safe and active sites. So encourage your readers to check them out!

INDEX